Hydrogen

Nigel Saunders

www.heinemann.co.uk/library

Visit our website to find out more information about Heinemann Library books.

To order:
☎ Phone 44 (0) 1865 888066
🖹 Send a fax to 44 (0) 1865 314091
🖥 Visit the Heinemann Bookshop at www.heinemann.co.uk/library to browse our catalogue and order online.

First published in Great Britain by Heinemann Library, Halley Court, Jordan Hill, Oxford OX2 8EJ, part of Harcourt Education.
Heinemann is a registered trademark of Harcourt Education Ltd.

Produced for Heinemann by Discovery Books Ltd.

Editorial: Dr Carol Usher and Sarah Eason
Design: Ian Winton
Illustrations: Stefan Chabluk
Picture Research: Vashti Gwynn
Production: Edward Moore

Originated by Ambassador Litho Ltd
Printed and bound in Hong Kong, China by South China Printing Company

ISBN 0 431 16998 5
07 06 05 04
10 9 8 7 6 5 4 3 2 1

British Library Cataloguing in Publication Data
Saunders, N. (Nigel)
    Hydrogen. – (The periodic table)
    - (The periodic table)
    546.2
A full catalogue record for this book is available from the British Library.

Acknowledgements
The publishers would like to thank the following for permission to reproduce photographs:
Corbis pp4 (George Lepp), 15 top, 17 (Bettmann), 16 (Hulton-Deutsch Collection), 18 (Kevin Fleming), 20 (Philip Gould), 23, 43 top (Ralph A Clevenger), 26 (RNT Productions), 27 (Caroline Penn), 30 (Ray Juno), 38 (Ted Spiegel), 43 bottom (Tecmap Corporation), 45 (Tom Stewart) Photography, 51 (Richard T Nowitz), 53 (Thom Lang) 56; NASA pp 11, 12, 22, 24, 55 bottom; Science Photo Library pp8 (Micheal Dunning), 13, 47 (Adam Hart-Davis), 15 bottom (Physics Department, Imperial College), 19 (Volker Steger), 28, 33, 41 (Charles D Winters), 29 (Martin Bond), 34, 35 (Andrew Lambert Photography), 48 (Pascal Goetgheluck), 49 (Astrid & Hans Frieder Michler), 50 (Dr Tim Evans), 55 top (David Frazier).

Cover photograph of a water droplet, reproduced with permission of Corbis.

The author would like to thank Angela, Kathryn, David and Jean for all their help and support.

Every effort has been made to contact copyright holders of any material reproduced in this book. Any omissions will be rectified in subsequent printings if notice is given to the publishers.

Contents

Words appearing in bold, **like this**, are explained in the Glossary

CHAPTER 1

Elements and atomic structure

Everything is made from chemicals, even you. Most chemicals are solids. However, some are gases, such as the air, and others are liquids, for instance water. Some chemicals are very big and complex, such as the proteins that make up your skin and hair, while others are simpler, such as the oxygen you need to stay alive. There are millions of different chemicals, which can be solid, liquid or gas, complex or simple, but they are all made from a few very basic substances called **elements**.

This is the start of a balloon race. Everything you can see here, including the balloons, vehicles and the people, is made from some of the millions of substances in the world. Some of the substances, like the oxygen in the hot air filling the balloons, will be elements but most will be compounds.

Elements and compounds

Elements are chemicals that cannot be broken down into simpler ones using chemical **reactions**. There are about ninety elements that occur naturally and scientists have learned how to make over twenty more using **nuclear reactions**. Most elements are metals, such as iron and magnesium, but some are non-metals, such as carbon and oxygen. Elements can join together in chemical reactions to make **compounds**. For instance, iron reacts with oxygen to make iron oxide, while carbon reacts with oxygen to form carbon dioxide. Most of the different chemicals in the world are compounds, made up of two or more elements chemically joined together.

Atoms

All chemicals are made up of tiny particles called **atoms**. Elements contain atoms that are all the same, while compounds are made from two or more types of atom joined together. Although we can see most of the chemicals around us, individual atoms are too tiny for us to see, even with a light microscope. Hydrogen is the simplest and smallest atom of all. It is about two and a half billion times smaller than a soccer ball.

Subatomic particles

Atoms are incredibly tiny, but they are made from even smaller objects called **subatomic particles**. At the centre of each atom there is a **nucleus**. This contains the biggest subatomic particles, which are called **protons** and **neutrons**. Arranged around the nucleus are even smaller subatomic particles called **electrons**. Subatomic particles are so minute that most of an atom is just empty space.

electron

nucleus of one proton

◄ *This is a model of an atom of hydrogen. The nucleus of each hydrogen atom usually contains one proton, although sometimes there are one or two neutrons as well. An electron is arranged in a shell, or energy level, around it.*

Groups

Elements react with each other in different ways, which makes chemistry very exciting. However to work out the reactions between the elements was a huge amount of work, so several people tried to organize them to make things easier. It was a Russian chemist called Dimitri Mendeleev who made the best attempt. In 1869, he made a table with eight **groups**, putting similar elements into each. Chemists found they could predict what would happen when they carried out chemical reactions and Mendeleev's table was so successful that it has evolved into the **periodic table** we use today.

CHAPTER 2

The periodic table and hydrogen

Chemists built on Mendeleev's work and produced the modern **periodic table**. Each row in the table is called a **period**. The **elements** in a period are arranged in order of increasing **atomic number** (number of **protons** in the **nucleus**). The columns in the table are called **groups** and there are eighteen. All the elements in each group have similar chemical properties to each other. It is called the periodic table because these different chemical properties occur regularly or periodically.

An element's properties are decided by the way its **electrons** are positioned around the nucleus. Electrons are arranged in shells, like layers of an onion. Each element in a group has the same number of electrons in the shell furthest from the nucleus, called the outer shell. For example all the elements in group 1 are very **reactive** metals and have one electron in their outer shells. The group 7 elements are very reactive non-metals and have seven electrons in their outer shells.

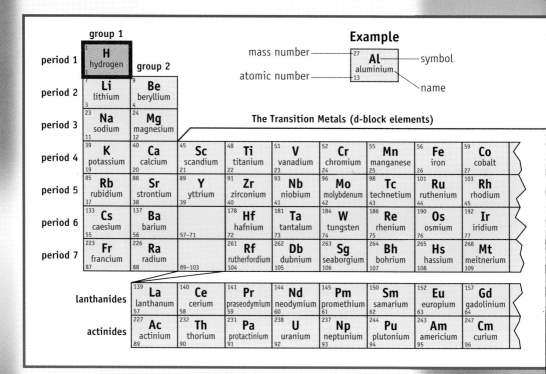

The properties of the elements change gradually as you go down a group. For example, the elements in group 7 become less reactive and their melting points increase. At the top of the group, fluorine and chlorine are both gases at room temperature. Fluorine is the most reactive element of all, even reacting with glass. Bromine, in the middle of the group, is the only non-metal element that is liquid at room temperature. Near the bottom of the group, iodine is solid at room temperature and is far less reactive than the three elements above it.

Hydrogen

Hydrogen only has one electron and this periodic table shows it above lithium in group 1, but hydrogen does not belong there at all because it has such different properties. In some periodic tables hydrogen is shown by itself. Hydrogen is a very special element and has many uses, as you will discover in this book.

▼ *This is the periodic table of the elements. Although hydrogen is often shown at the top of group 1, it does not belong to the group because it is a non-metal and very different from the metallic elements in group 1.*

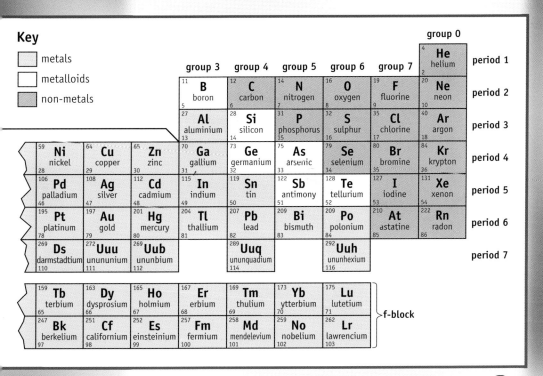

CHAPTER 3

Hydrogen right from the start

Nobody was around when the Universe began, so it is difficult to be certain what happened. However, scientists have gathered evidence about the Universe and how it works. They have used this evidence to describe in detail how they think the Universe started and then developed. Their theory is called the Big Bang and it seems that hydrogen was there almost from the very beginning.

Too hot to handle

The Universe started off as something incredibly tiny and hot around 13,700 million years ago. In the Big Bang, there was a massive explosion and the Universe expanded very quickly and began to cool down. The temperature of the Universe at this time was more than we can imagine. A Bunsen burner can get to about 1000 °C, but about a hundredth of a second after the Big Bang the temperature of the Universe was about 100,000,000,000 °C! All sorts of tiny particles appeared and disappeared in a fiery soup that was full of energy and **radiation**. **Protons** and **neutrons** formed as the Universe continued to cool, but it was still too hot for them to stick together to make the **nuclei** of **atoms**.

At the centre of every atom there is a nucleus. If we want to talk about more than one nucleus, we say nuclei (pronounced 'new-clee-eye').

Protons and neutrons

Protons and neutrons are even smaller than atoms and very much lighter. A proton is so light that six hundred thousand million million million of them would only have a mass of one gram! Obviously this makes it really difficult to discuss their masses sensibly. Protons and neutrons are almost identical in mass, so we use a relative scale to compare their masses more easily. If we call the mass of a proton 1, the mass of a neutron is also 1.

From nothing to three nuclei in three minutes!

Scientists believe the Universe kept on cooling very quickly after the Big Bang and after about three minutes it had cooled to about 1,000,000,000 °C. This was cold enough for protons and neutrons to stick together to make the nuclei of atoms. Over 90 per cent of the nuclei were hydrogen nuclei, made from just one proton or a proton with one or two neutrons stuck on. The rest were mostly helium nuclei, each made from two protons and two neutrons stuck together. There were also a few lithium nuclei, each made from three protons and four neutrons.

Electrons were also whizzing around the Universe, but before they could slow down enough to stay with the nuclei to form atoms the Universe had to cool down even more.

◀ *This artwork simulates the Big Bang theory. Scientists believe that our Universe began as something incredibly tiny and exploded outwards about 13,700 million years ago (opposite). Hydrogen, helium and lithium atoms were the first atoms formed as the Universe became bigger and cooler.*

Atoms everywhere!

Hundreds of thousands of years passed before the Universe cooled down enough for the first **electrons** to stay with **nuclei** to make **atoms**, but when they did, about three-quarters of them were hydrogen.

Attractive electrons

Neutrons have no electrical charge, but **protons** are positively charged. Electrons are negatively charged, so they are strongly attracted to the positive protons in a nucleus. However, electrons only began to stay with nuclei when the Universe had cooled to 3000 °C. Once this happened, about three hundred thousand years after the Big Bang, atoms started to form. About a million years after the Big Bang, all the nuclei had joined with electrons to make atoms.

The three subatomic particles

Here are the properties of protons, neutrons and electrons.

particle	relative mass	relative charge	position in atoms
proton	1	+1	nucleus
neutron	1	0	nucleus
electron	$1/1836$	-1	shells

Electrons and protons have opposite charges. However, their electrical charges are the same size, even though electrons are nearly two thousand times lighter than protons.

Hydrogen in the Universe

Most hydrogen atoms are made from just one proton with one electron arranged around it. However, some hydrogen atoms also contain one or two neutrons. Atoms that have the same number of protons and electrons, but different numbers of neutrons are called **isotopes**.

This is the centre of the Orion nebula (opposite), seen through the Hubble Space Telescope. Hundreds of new stars are forming inside the nebula's gigantic swirling mass of gas and dust. ▶

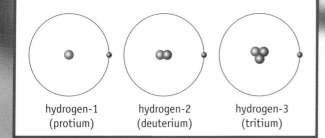

hydrogen-1
(protium)

hydrogen-2
(deuterium)

hydrogen-3
(tritium)

▲

These are models of the three hydrogen isotopes. Each atom contains just one proton and one electron, but the nucleus of hydrogen-2 also has a neutron while the nucleus of hydrogen-3 contains two neutrons.

Most hydrogen isotopes are hydrogen-1 (protium) and have one proton but no neutrons in their nuclei. Atoms of hydrogen-2 (deuterium) have one proton and one neutron. While atoms of hydrogen-3 (tritium) have one proton and two neutrons. All three isotopes **react** the same way chemically because they have identical numbers of protons and electrons. However, they have different masses and some can be **radioactive**.

The first stars

Over millions of years, gravity gradually pulled atoms together to form big clumps. Really big clumps eventually formed stars. About two hundred million years after the Big Bang the first stars lit up.

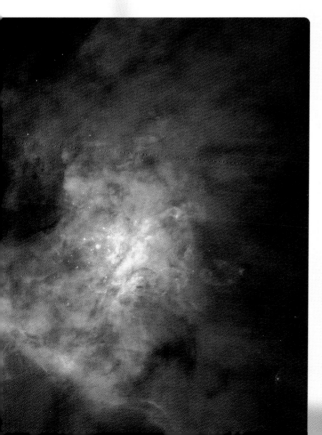

A star uses a type of **nuclear reaction** called nuclear fusion to produce its heated light. In a star, this involves hydrogen nuclei joining together to make helium nuclei, producing a tremendous amount of energy. Gravity pulls the star together and stops it exploding. However, as it gets older a star begins to run out of hydrogen and starts to shrink. Other nuclei join together and make the nuclei of new **elements**. Stars may shrink so fast that they explode, triggering a supernova. This causes material, containing lots of elements, to shoot out into space.

Star dust

Planets in the Solar System contain **elements** that come from the star dust produced by supernovae. The **atoms** in food that we eat, air we breathe and the water we drink come from this star dust – even we do!

The Milky Way

Galaxies are clusters of billions of stars and there may be over a hundred billion galaxies in the Universe. Our galaxy is called the Milky Way and contains over a hundred billion stars, but one star near the edge is really important to us because it is our Sun. The Earth and the other planets in the Solar System go round the Sun.

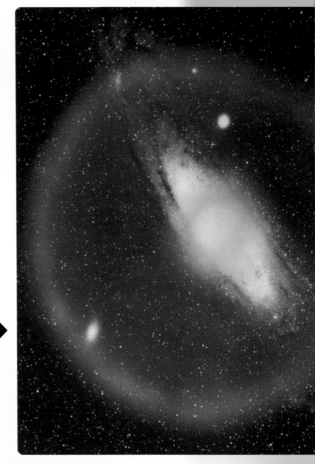

Galaxies come in many different shapes and sizes, including spinning discs like our own Milky Way. The Milky Way contains our own Sun and over a hundred billion other stars. ▶

The Solar System

The Solar System began as a huge cloud of dust and gas in space, containing elements made in earlier stars. Gravity began to pull the cloud together and a spinning disc of material formed. The material in the cloud began to spiral inwards, a bit like the way that water spirals down a plug hole. It got hotter as it did this and eventually became so hot that **nuclear reactions** started. As a result, the Sun was born about 5000 million years ago. The planets formed about 4600 million years ago from the remains of the cloud of dust and gas. The planets closest to the Sun (Mercury, Venus, Earth and Mars) are rocky, while those further away are made of gas. The Earth is the only planet in the Solar System to have large amounts of liquid water.

Where's all the hydrogen?

Hydrogen is the most abundant atom in the Universe, in our Sun and in seawater. It has the lightest atoms of all, which is why there are big differences between the two columns in the table below. Silicon and oxygen are the two most abundant elements in the Earth's crust and together form 69 per cent of its atoms.

This table shows the proportions of hydrogen in the Universe, our Sun, the Earth's crust and seawater.

	Per cent of atoms	Per cent of mass
Universe	93.0	76.0
Our Sun	93.0	76.0
Earth's crust	3.1	0.1
Seawater	66.2	10.7

Hydrogen on Earth

Hydrogen is only about the tenth most abundant atom in the Earth's crust. Hydrogen atoms usually join together to make hydrogen **molecules**, H_2. Each hydrogen molecule contains two hydrogen atoms, joined together by a chemical **bond**. The Earth's atmosphere contains very little hydrogen gas because it can easily escape into space. Luckily for us, most hydrogen atoms are joined with oxygen atoms to make water molecules. Each water molecule, H_2O, is made from two hydrogen atoms and one oxygen atom, joined together by chemical bonds.

▲
*Chemists often make models of molecules to help them explain the **reactions** they study. This is a model of a water molecule, H_2O. The white balls represent hydrogen atoms and the red ball represents an oxygen atom.*

CHAPTER 4

Inflammable air

The properties of hydrogen

Hydrogen is a colourless gas with no smell and it is not poisonous. It does not dissolve very well in water; only eighteen litres or 1.5g of it dissolves in a cubic metre of water at room temperature. Hydrogen is a very **reactive element**; if a spark or flame is put into a mixture of hydrogen and air, the hydrogen reacts with the oxygen in the air and explodes.

The pop test for hydrogen
There is a simple laboratory test for hydrogen. The test relies on the reaction between hydrogen and oxygen in air. If a lighted wooden splint is put inside a test tube of hydrogen, the hydrogen burns very quickly and makes a popping sound. It can be really loud and squeaky if some air is let in first!

Hydrogen also explodes when mixed with very reactive gases such as fluorine and chlorine. It reacts with hot metal oxides and removes the oxygen from them. These reactions form water, which is hydrogen oxide, leaving the metal behind.

The word equation for copper oxide reacting with hydrogen is:

$$\text{copper oxide} + \text{hydrogen} \xrightarrow{\text{heat}} \text{copper} + \text{hydrogen oxide (water)}$$

The discovery of hydrogen

Hydrogen is easily made by mixing metals and acids together, so hydrogen was actually discovered many times. However, most chemists did not realize that they had discovered a new element. They thought it was a type of air and was often called inflammable air. The word 'inflammable' has the same meaning as 'flammable' – something that is easily set on fire.

Henry Cavendish, an English chemist, finally discovered that inflammable air was really an element in 1766. In 1783, a French chemist called Antoine Lavoisier discovered that water is the only substance made when inflammable air burns in air. Although Cavendish discovered hydrogen, it was Lavoisier who named it. The word hydrogen comes from the Greek words 'hydro genes', meaning 'water-forming'.

◀ The French chemist Antoine Lavoisier (1743 – 1794) discovered that hydrogen and oxygen react together to make water. Lavoisier (who is in the middle of this engraving) is seen here showing other scientists one of his experiments on the different gases in air.

Traces of hydrogen in sunlight

Anders Ångström, a Swedish physicist, discovered hydrogen in the Sun in 1862 by studying sunlight. The Sun produces light containing all the colours of the **spectrum**, although not all of them reach us. The hydrogen in the Sun absorbs some of the colours, leaving tell-tale black lines in its spectrum. When hydrogen burns it produces its own spectrum. Ångström compared the missing colours in sunlight with the spectrum produced by hydrogen and realized that they matched exactly.

▼ Scientists can work out which elements are in the Sun by studying its spectrum. Different elements absorb different colours in the spectrum, producing thousands of black lines. The line in the yellow part is caused by sodium.

Into the air with hydrogen

Helium is often used to lift party balloons into the air because it has a low **density**, but hydrogen has the lowest density of any of the **elements**. A litre of helium has a mass of 0.166 g, twice the mass of the same volume of hydrogen. This means that hydrogen should be even better than helium for lifting party balloons. However, there is a big problem with using hydrogen, as you will discover.

Getting balloons to go up

A litre of air weighs 1.2 g, while a litre of hydrogen weighs just 0.083 g – over a gram less! If the hydrogen's container weighed less than a gram, it would float upwards! Balloons are light enough to float when filled with hydrogen. A small balloon, 0.3 m in diameter, could lift about 16 g including the mass of the balloon. This may not sound like a lot, but a really big balloon can lift a huge weight. Barrage balloons, enormous balloons filled with over 500 cubic metres of hydrogen, were used in World War II to make it more difficult for enemy aircraft to fly over towns and cities. However, even these were tiny compared to the great airships.

Barrage balloons ▶
like these made
things very difficult
for enemy aircraft in
World War II. They were
20 m long and 9 m high and were
filled with hydrogen.

The *Hindenburg*

The *Hindenburg* was a huge airship designed by a German called Count von Zeppelin. It was 245 m long, more than three times the length of a modern Boeing 747 airliner. The airship was kept in the air by 200,000 cubic metres of hydrogen and could carry fifty crew, seventy-two passengers and eleven tonnes of cargo. The *Hindenburg* went into service carrying passengers between Europe and the USA, but a terrible disaster awaited it at Lakehurst in New Jersey in 1937.

The Hindenburg *was an enormous airship filled with hydrogen. While coming in to land on 6 May 1937, a spark caused by static electricity set its skin on fire. The hydrogen gas expanded and burst out of its containers, causing the* Hindenburg *to explode in a huge fireball.*

While trying to land at Lakehurst, the *Hindenburg* suddenly burst into flames. It was completely destroyed, killing many of the people on board. The huge amount of flammable hydrogen it was carrying got the blame for the explosion. After this accident and others, airships went out of fashion for a long time. Modern airships are much smaller and are lifted by helium rather than hydrogen. Unlike hydrogen, helium is not **reactive** and cannot ignite or explode.

Was hydrogen to blame?

Although hydrogen was blamed for starting the fire in the *Hindenburg*, aluminium may have been the culprit. The *Hindenburg's* frame was covered with a fabric treated with a mixture of aluminium powder and iron oxide. This mixture is also called thermit and it is used to **weld** railway lines. When it catches fire, thermit reacts very fiercely with huge flames, producing aluminium oxide and iron. It gets so hot that the iron melts!

Liquid hydrogen

Hydrogen condenses to form a liquid at −253 °C. Liquid hydrogen is over sixty times **denser** than hydrogen gas, so you can fit more of it into a container. This is useful if hydrogen is being used as a fuel, but the very low temperatures needed bring their own problems.

Cryogenics

The coldest temperature possible is −273.15 °C. This is called absolute zero. The temperature of liquid hydrogen is only 20 °C above this, so it really is incredibly cold. Ordinary refrigerators cannot reach temperatures like these, so special 'cryogenic' refrigerators are needed. These machines require a lot of energy just to run. Many substances become brittle and break easily at these low temperatures, so special containers are needed to store and transport the liquid hydrogen. It might seem that liquid hydrogen is too tricky to bother with, but it is very useful for scientific research and powering rockets.

Bubble chambers

Subatomic particles such as **protons**, **neutrons** and **electrons** are far too small to see. There are other subatomic particles too, which physicists are keen to study. Although these particles are not visible, it is possible to see where they have been, using a device called a bubble chamber.

The bubble chamber contains liquid hydrogen that is pressurized so it is on the verge of boiling. Wherever subatomic particles pass through the liquid hydrogen, they give it just enough extra energy to boil. This produces a trail of tiny hydrogen gas bubbles, which follows the particles. The physicists photograph the trails to help them with their research.

Liquid hydrogen is used in bubble chambers. These devices allow scientists to study the strange spiral paths taken by tiny subatomic particles. ▶

Into space with liquid hydrogen

Car manufacturers are experimenting with liquid hydrogen as a fuel for cars. Although it is difficult to store and handle, scientists are confident they can overcome any problems. However, rockets and spacecraft have used liquid hydrogen as a fuel for many years.

This technician is working on the fuel tank in a car powered by hydrogen. The tank contains liquid hydrogen at −253 °C and is insulated with seventy layers of aluminium and fibreglass.

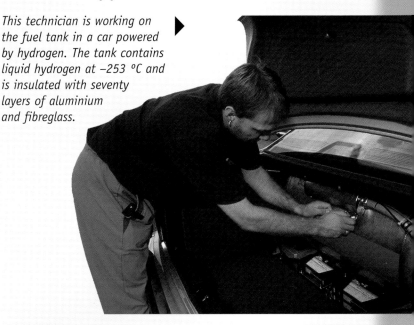

The Space Shuttles use liquid hydrogen to power their main engines. The huge external tank attached to the Shuttle at lift-off contains one and half million litres of it. There are also half a million litres of liquid oxygen stored inside the nose of the tank. The two liquids are pumped to the engines where they are mixed and ignited, producing huge forces that push the shuttle into space. The tank itself is made from a very strong, but light, aluminium-lithium **alloy**.

Cold cracks

The Shuttle fleet was grounded for repairs in 2002. Very small cracks were found in the tubes that supply liquid hydrogen to the engines. These could cause a piece of metal to come off the tubes and destroy the engines. No cracks were found in the tubes supplying the liquid oxygen and it seemed that the extreme cold of the liquid hydrogen was to blame.

A hydrogen economy

Hydrogen is easy to set alight and burns with a hot flame. A small amount of hydrogen releases a lot of energy – nearly three times more than the same mass of natural gas or petrol. Hydrogen has other advantages too, but there are some disadvantages.

Environmentally friendly hydrogen

Fossil fuels, such as natural gas and petrol, produce carbon dioxide and water when they burn. However, the only **product** when hydrogen burns is water vapour. This gives hydrogen a big advantage over fossil fuels because carbon dioxide is a 'greenhouse' gas that traps heat in the atmosphere and contributes to global warming. However, we still use fossil fuels, despite this advantage because hydrogen is difficult to transport and store safely.

Hydrogen for homes and cars

Hydrogen gas could be piped to homes for heating and cooking, just like natural gas. However, this is not practical for cars. If hydrogen gas is stored under pressure, more gas can be squeezed into a small volume. Unfortunately, special containers are needed to do this.

If hydrogen gas is cooled below −253 °C, it condenses and becomes a liquid. However, around a quarter of the energy contained in the hydrogen would be used just to keep it that cold and special containers are still needed for storage. Despite these problems, hydrogen is already being used to power vehicles.

Metal hydrides

One possible answer to the problems of storing hydrogen safely and cheaply involves metal hydrides. These are produced when some metals **react** with hydrogen. **Alloys**, such as magnesium-nickel and magnesium-copper, can store large amounts of hydrogen this way. When the metal hydrides are heated, they release the hydrogen gas. However, more scientific research is needed to increase the amount of hydrogen they can store.

The hydrogen fuel cell

In 1842, an English scientist called Sir William Grove invented the 'gas battery'. Grove's invention consisted of two strips of platinum metal half-covered by sulphuric acid. He discovered that electricity was produced if hydrogen was passed over one strip and oxygen over the other. The 'gas battery' is the basis of the modern hydrogen fuel cell.

The hydrogen fuel cell produces electricity from hydrogen and oxygen when it is supplied in a steady stream. The only product is water vapour, making it very attractive as an environmentally friendly power source. The International Space Station uses fuel cells to make electricity, and drinking water is a useful by-product for the astronauts. Back on Earth, hydrogen fuel cells are being used to power cars and other vehicles. The electricity they generate charges a battery, which powers an electric motor.

◄ *Oil and natural gas produce water and carbon dioxide (a greenhouse gas) when they burn. They may also produce black smoke (opposite). However, when hydrogen burns the only product is water vapour.*

CHAPTER 5

Hydrogen oxide

When hydrogen and oxygen **react** together, the only **product** is water. Water, H_2O, is hydrogen oxide. Like all **compounds**, water is very different from the **elements** it contains. Hydrogen and oxygen are both gases at room temperature, whereas water is a liquid. Pure water freezes at 0 °C and boils at 100 °C. It is colourless and does not smell. Tap water usually smells faintly of chlorine because chlorine is added to kill harmful bacteria.

Hydrogen oxide, better known as water, is the most abundant compound on the surface of the Earth. As a result, our home planet, when seen from space is a very watery place covered with oceans and clouds. ▶

Water is the most abundant compound on Earth, and covers 71 per cent of the Earth's surface. There are about one thousand four hundred million cubic kilometres of water on Earth. This is so much that if each person in the world scooped out a litre of water every second, it would take seven thousand years to drain the oceans!

It's a liquid, but is it water?

There are two simple chemical tests to see if a liquid is water. If it is added to very dry copper sulphate crystals, they change from white to blue. Paper soaked in cobalt chloride solution can also be used as a test for water. Cobalt chloride paper is blue when dry, but turns pink when it is damp with water. Even the moisture from your fingers is enough to change its colour.

Burst pipes

Most substances contract when they change from a liquid to a solid, but water expands when it freezes. A kilogram of water has a volume of 1.00 litre, but ice expands and fills 1.09 litres. If water freezes in a pipe, it not only blocks it, but expands and pushes against the inside of the pipe, causing it to split. When the weather becomes warmer, the ice melts, unblocking the pipe and water leaks out of the split.

Icebergs

Ice is less **dense** than water, which is why ice cubes float in a drink. The density of pure water is 1.00 g/cm^3 but seawater can be nearly 1.03 g/cm^3 because it contains dissolved salt. Meanwhile, the density of icebergs varies from just 0.86 g/cm3 to 0.92 g/cm3, so they float in the sea. About 90 per cent of an iceberg is under water and many ships, including the famous *Titanic*, have collided with sharp bits of iceberg under their water line and sunk.

▼ *People often talk about things being 'just the tip of the iceberg'. Ice is less dense than water, so it floats, but only about 10 per cent of an iceberg is visible on the surface.*

Water the dissolver

Water is a good solvent, which means that many substances dissolve in it easily. All sorts of substances will dissolve in water, such as sugar and sodium chloride (common salt). On average, every litre of seawater contains twenty-six grams of dissolved sodium chloride, thirty-five thousand trillion tonnes in all the Earth's seas and oceans.

Water everywhere

When the Earth was first formed it was very hot indeed. Volcanoes threw huge amounts of gases such as carbon dioxide and steam into the sky. Eventually the Earth's temperature cooled to below 100 °C and the steam condensed to form liquid water, which fell as rain and formed the oceans.

Scientists believe that similar things happened on Venus and Mars, but neither planet has liquid water now. Venus is closer to the Sun than Earth and it is too hot there for steam to condense. It is likely that chemical **reactions** split the water **molecules** into hydrogen and oxygen gas. Hydrogen has very small molecules that can move extremely quickly and they probably escaped into space. Mars is further away from the Sun than we are and is too cold for liquid water. However space probes have discovered some frozen water under the surface. Scientists believe that Mars had oceans, rivers and floods over three billion years ago, before it cooled.

▲
This is the Valles Marineris canyon on Mars, which scientists believe was carved out by water millions of years ago. Although there is no flowing water on Mars now, the Mars Odyssey space probe discovered in 2003 that the soil on Mars contains an average of 6.5 per cent water.

Before the ozone layer
The Earth's ozone layer protects living things from harmful ultraviolet light. Before it formed four hundred million years ago, life could only exist in the oceans. This is because seawater gives some protection from the Sun's ultraviolet light.

The water cycle

The Earth's water is continually moving and changing. Water evaporates from the surface of lakes and seas, forming water vapour. This rises into the sky and becomes cooler. As the water vapour cools, it condenses into clouds of tiny water droplets. When the clouds cool further, like they do when they rise over mountains, the droplets clump together, eventually becoming large enough to fall as rain. Most rain just falls back into the sea, but about a fifth of it falls over the land. It then flows back to the sea over ground as rivers and underground as groundwater. These processes are driven by heat energy from the Sun, forming the water cycle. The water in the atmosphere of the Earth is recycled thirty-three times every year!

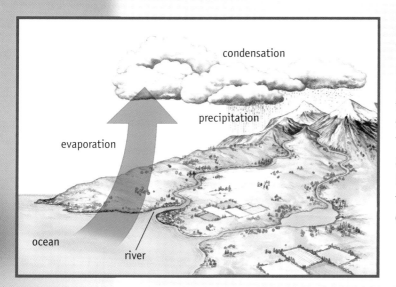

▲
This diagram shows the water cycle, in which water is continually recycled between the oceans, clouds and land. The water cycle is driven by heat energy from the Sun.

Swimming pools and mild weather

Water has a high heat capacity. This means that a large amount of energy is needed to warm water up, making swimming pools expensive to heat. On the other hand, warm water stores a lot of heat energy, so oceans and seas have a large effect on the sort of weather we get. They absorb heat in the summer and release it in the winter, preventing large swings in temperature. For instance, the average yearly temperatures in the UK, which is an island, only vary by about 10 °C. North America and Europe, on the other hand, are large continents and areas away from the sea can have average yearly temperatures that vary by as much as 40 °C.

Water and living things

Without water, the Earth would be a lifeless planet. About 60 per cent of our body mass is water and we can only survive a few days without it.

Photosynthesis and respiration

Plants make their own food using a process called photosynthesis. Energy from sunlight enables carbon dioxide and water to **react** together to produce sugar and oxygen. If a plant does not get enough water, its cells become floppy. The plant wilts and may eventually die.

Respiration is the chemical reaction that all cells use to release energy from food. Water is a **product** of respiration and our bodies get rid of extra water by sweating or going to the toilet. Our breath contains water vapour, which we can see when it condenses in the cold air as we breathe out. Without respiration we could not get the energy we need for our bodies to move, grow and keep warm.

Water is vital for us to stay alive. We usually take safe and clean drinking water for granted, but in many parts of the world it is very difficult to get. ▶

Germination

Seeds may seem to be dead, but they are just dormant. This means that all the chemical processes in their cells, such as respiration, are happening very slowly. When seeds are sown into damp soil, they soak up water. The cells begin to respire more quickly and the seed germinates. The germinating seeds use their store of food to produce roots and shoots, forming new plants. Without water, seeds cannot germinate.

Fresh water

Although there is a fantastic amount of water on Earth, about 97 per cent of it is seawater and very little of the remainder is fit for us to drink. Most of it is locked away as ice in glaciers and icebergs or below ground as groundwater. Nearly all our drinking water comes from rivers and they only contain 0.0001 per cent of the world's water! The rivers also supply the water needed for industrial processes, such as steel-making. Over two hundred tonnes of water are used to make each tonne of steel.

Clean water

To survive, we each need about five litres of water a day from our food and drink, but we use at least ten times that for other purposes such as washing. In the developed world, it is easy to take the supply of clean water for granted, but over a billion people in the world cannot get it. Contaminated water causes over four billion cases of diarrhoea each year, killing over two million people. Many tropical diseases are spread by parasites that live in untreated water. Schistosomiasis (pronounced 'shis-toe-so-my-a-siss') is a tropical disease caused by tiny worms that live in the veins around the liver and intestines. People become infected if they touch infested water, for example, when they irrigate fields, collect drinking water, wash themselves or go swimming. About two hundred million people are infected, mainly in central and southern Africa. In 2002, the World Summit for Sustainable Development agreed to take steps to halve the proportion of people without safe drinking water by 2015.

◀ Clean running water is difficult to find in some developing countries and war zones, so people may have to travel many kilometres to collect water. Even then, it may be dirty and capable of causing fatal diseases such as cholera.

Water and electricity

The electric battery was invented by an Italian scientist called Alessandro Volta. When he announced his invention in 1800, chemists rushed to find out what would happen when electricity is passed through chemicals. One of the first chemicals they tested was water.

Only a few months after Volta announced his invention an English chemist, called William Nicholson, discovered that water splits into hydrogen and oxygen when electricity is passed through. It is incredibly dangerous to pass mains electricity through water and you must never try this at home. Pure water is a poor conductor of electricity unless large voltages are applied, but it conducts better if it contains some impurities.

The electrolysis of water

When electricity is used to split up a **compound** into simpler substances, the process is called electrolysis. Water is a compound made from hydrogen and oxygen **atoms**. Water **molecules** split up to make hydrogen **ions**, H^+ and hydroxide ions, OH^-. Ions are electrically charged particles, so the hydrogen ions are attracted to the negative electrode, becoming hydrogen gas. The hydroxide ions are attracted to the positive electrode, where they **react** with each other to form oxygen gas and water.

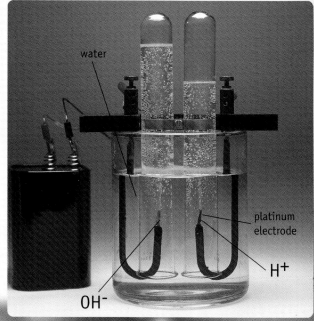

water

platinum electrode

H^+

OH^-

Water can be split into hydrogen and oxygen using electricity from a battery. The gases bubble out of the water into test tubes, where they can be collected. The test tube on the right contains hydrogen and the one on the left contains oxygen.

The word equation for the electrolysis of water is:

$$\text{water} \xrightarrow{\text{electricity}} \text{hydrogen} + \text{oxygen}$$

Twice as much hydrogen is made compared to oxygen because each water molecule has two hydrogen atoms, but only one oxygen atom.

Industrial hydrogen

Most hydrogen is **extracted** by reacting steam with coal or natural gas. Unfortunately, these reactions also produce carbon dioxide gas, which is a contributor to global warming. In addition coal and natural gas are both **fossil fuels** that will run out one day. Obtaining hydrogen through the electrolysis of water is a good alternative, although electricity is expensive to produce and is often generated from fossil fuels too.

Solar cells convert the Sun's light directly into electricity. Electricity can also be generated using alternative energy sources such as hydroelectric power, wind and waves. The cost of electricity will come down when these alternative sources become more widely used and then the electrolysis of water will be a more economic way of extracting hydrogen.

◀ This wave power station on the Scottish island of Islay generates electricity cheaply. Inexpensive electricity is needed to make the electrolysis of hydrogen economic.

Hydrogen from the chlor-alkali industry

Hydrogen is a by-product of the chlor-alkali industry. This chemical industry extracts chlorine and sodium hydroxide (an alkali, see page 32) by passing electricity through sodium chloride solution.

Corrosive hydrogen

Acids

When acids dissolve in water they make acidic solutions. All acids contain hydrogen **atoms**, which give off hydrogen gas when they **react** with metals. Vinegar is a weak acid that contains ethanoic acid, CH_3COOH, while lemon juice has citric acid, $C_6H_8O_7$. Our stomachs contain hydrochloric acid, HCl, which is a strong acid and kills harmful bacteria in our food as well as helping us to digest proteins. There are also strong acids in car batteries (sulphuric acid, H_2SO_4) and in cola drinks (phosphoric acid, H_3PO_4). This is why cola drinks dissolve our teeth.

Lemons like these, and other citrus fruits, contain a weak acid called citric acid. ▶

◀ *Bottles of very strong or concentrated acids are labelled with this hazard symbol. It warns us that the chemical is corrosive and can attack living tissues such as the skin or eyes.*

Weak or diluted acids are less dangerous than strong or concentrated acids, but they can still harm us if they are spilt on our skin or swallowed. This hazard symbol warns us if a chemical is an irritant. ▶

Fizzing furiously

Metals react with acids to produce a **salt** and hydrogen.

> *The word equation for the reaction between a metal and an acid is:*
>
> metal + acid → salt + hydrogen

> *These are some examples of reactions between metals and acids. See how the salt gets its name.*
>
> zinc + sulphuric acid → zinc sulphate + hydrogen
>
> magnesium + hydrochloric acid → magnesium chloride + hydrogen

The names of salts are a bit like our own names – they have a first name and a last name. The first name is the name of the metal and the last name comes from the acid used. For example, the last name is nitrate if nitric acid is used and phosphate if phosphoric acid is used. When a salt is made with hydrochloric acid, the last part of the salt's name is chloride.

element	
	most reactive
potassium	
sodium	
lithium	
calcium	
magnesium	
aluminium	
zinc	
iron	
tin	
lead	
hydrogen	
copper	
silver	
gold	
platinum	least reactive

Metals can be arranged in order of their reactivity to make a list called a reactivity series. Metals above hydrogen react with acids, while those below normally do not. The more reactive the metal, the bigger the reaction. For example, you could make table salt, or sodium chloride, by reacting sodium with hydrochloric acid, but the reaction would be violent because sodium is very reactive! To make it safely, you need a different type of substance, called a base.

◀ *A reactivity series of metals with hydrogen included.*

Bases and alkalis

Bases are substances that **react** with acids and **neutralize** them, so they are no longer acidic. If a base dissolves in water, it is also called an alkali. This means that all alkalis are bases, but not all bases are alkalis. Copper oxide powder is a base because it neutralizes acids. It also dissolves in water, so it is an alkali.

Back to base

Lots of substances are bases, including ammonia, metal oxides such as copper oxide and metal hydroxides such as sodium hydroxide. Metal carbonates and metal hydrogencarbonates are bases, too. These include substances such as calcium carbonate that is found in chalk and limestone, and sodium hydrogencarbonate, which is part of baking powder.

Alkali and alkaline

For thousands of years people have burned plants and boiled their ashes in water to produce an alkaline solution. The word 'alkali' comes from 'al-qali', the Arabic words for burned ashes. Potassium hydroxide, KOH, is a common alkali. Potassium gets its name from 'potash', literally the ashes from a pot! People sometimes get alkali and alkaline muddled up. Remember that acids dissolve in water to make acidic solutions and alkalis dissolve in water to make alkaline solutions. Boiling fats and oils in an alkaline solution makes soap.

Soapy alkalis

Alkalis must be handled carefully as they are corrosive or harmful, like acids. Alkalis react with the natural oils in your skin to produce soap, which is why they feel soapy! However, alkalis can cause nasty burns, so they must be washed off your skin and clothes. They are particularly dangerous if they get into your eyes so you must wear eye protection when you do experiments with alkalis.

Bases and salts

A **salt** is always produced when a base reacts with an acid and is named in the same way as a salt made from a metal and an acid. For example, sodium chloride is made from the reaction between sodium hydroxide and hydrochloric acid. The other chemicals produced depend on the type of base used. Water will be formed if the base is a metal oxide or hydroxide, while water and carbon dioxide will be produced if a metal carbonate or hydrogencarbonate is used.

The word equations for the reactions between different bases and acids are:

metal oxide + acid → salt + water

metal hydroxide + acid → salt + water

metal carbonate + acid → salt + water + carbon dioxide

metal hydrogencarbonate + acid → salt + water + carbon dioxide

When ammonia solution reacts with an acid, the first part of the name for the salt formed is 'ammonium'. For instance, ammonia solution reacts with hydrochloric acid to make ammonium chloride and water.

◀ *Acids and alkalis react together to form a salt and water. When the fumes from concentrated hydrochloric acid meet the fumes from ammonia solution, they react to form clouds of white ammonium chloride and water vapour.*

Indicators and the pH scale

There are several different ways to find out if a solution is acidic or alkaline.

Indicators

Indicators are substances that can tell us whether a solution is acidic, alkaline or neutral by their colour. Litmus is an indicator that is **extracted** from lichens. Lichens are members of the plant kingdom formed from a fungus and an alga, which grow on tree trunks and rocks. Litmus solution turns red in acids and blue in alkalis. Universal indicator is a mixture of different indicators. It not only turns red in acids and blue in alkalis, but it turns green in neutral solutions and shows you the strength of an acidic or alkaline solution.

Litmus paper v universal indicator paper

This table shows the colour changes made by indicator papers in different solutions.

	acidic	neutral	alkaline
red litmus paper	stays red	stays red	turns blue
blue litmus paper	turns red	stays blue	stays blue
universal indicator paper	turns red	turns green	turns blue

Litmus paper is not as useful as universal indicator paper. You may need both a red and a blue piece to be sure of your result and litmus paper cannot tell you if an acid or alkali is strong or weak.

◀ *Blue litmus paper turns red when it soaks up the acidic juice from a lemon.*

The pH scale

The pH scale is a measure of acidity. It runs from 0 to 14. Solutions that have pH numbers less than 7 are acidic, while alkaline solutions have pH numbers more than 7. The pH number of neutral solutions is 7 exactly. Strong acids have pH numbers close to 0 and strong alkalis have pH numbers near to 14. Weak acids and alkalis have pH numbers close to 7. Pure water is neutral.

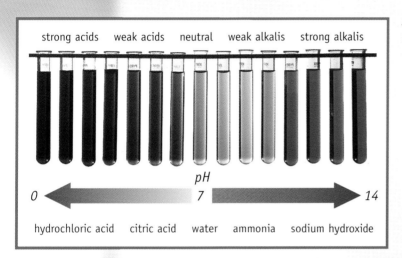

The solutions in these test tubes show the universal indicator pH scale.

The pH value of a solution can be found using universal indicator paper and a colour chart, where each colour is given a pH number. A device called a pH meter can also be used. A probe is put into the liquid to be tested and the pH number is read on the scale.

Neutralization and the pH scale

When a base **neutralizes** an acid, it is called a neutralization **reaction**. It is the reaction between hydrogen **ions** from the acid and hydroxide ions from the base. These ions join together to form water. The pH scale is an inverse measure of the amount of hydrogen ions dissolved in the solution. This means strong acids produce a lot of hydrogen ions, giving a low pH number.

The word equation for the neutralization reaction is:

hydrogen ions + hydroxide ions → water

Caves and cooking

Limestone and chalk are almost pure forms of calcium carbonate, $CaCO_3$. Calcium carbonate is a base, so it can **react** with acids and **neutralize** them. You can test a rock to see if calcium carbonate is present by adding a few drops of hydrochloric acid. If it contains limestone or chalk, the rock immediately begins to fizz. This is because the reaction produces carbon dioxide gas.

> *The word equation for the reaction between calcium carbonate and hydrochloric acid is:*
>
> $$\text{calcium carbonate} + \text{hydrochloric acid} \rightarrow \text{calcium chloride} + \text{water} + \text{carbon dioxide}$$

Rainwater is naturally acidic because carbon dioxide in the air dissolves in it, forming a weak acid, called carbonic acid, H_2CO_3. When rainwater falls on to limestone or chalk, it reacts with the calcium carbonate, producing calcium hydrogencarbonate, which can dissolve in water. This causes the rock to wear away and over thousands of years channels and caves are formed. When water that contains calcium hydrogencarbonate drips from cave ceilings it evaporates, leaving behind stalactites and stalagmites of calcium carbonate.

> *The word equation for the reaction between calcium carbonate and carbonic acid is:*
>
> $$\text{calcium carbonate} + \text{carbonic acid} \rightleftharpoons \text{calcium hydrogencarbonate}$$
>
> *This is a reversible reaction, because calcium hydrogencarbonate can break down again to form calcium carbonate and carbonic acid. Instead of the usual arrow, we use the $\rightleftharpoons$ symbol.*

Acid rain

Cars and factories produce polluting gases that include sulphur dioxide and nitrogen oxides or NOx. These gases dissolve in the clouds and the rain that later falls from them is more acidic than normal. Acid rain is very damaging to statues and buildings made from limestone or marble.

Baking soda

Sodium hydrogencarbonate, $NaHCO_3$, is often called 'baking soda' or 'bicarbonate of soda'. It dissolves in water to form a weak alkaline solution. Some toothpastes contain baking soda, which help to neutralize acid made by bacteria in our mouths from the sugars in our food. The tiny baking soda crystals also help to clean our teeth.

Baking soda breaks down when it is heated and releases carbon dioxide gas. This helps cakes to rise in the oven. Baking soda is often mixed with a dry acid such as tartaric acid to make 'baking powder'. When baking powder is put into a damp cake mixture, the sodium hydrogen carbonate and tartic acid react and release carbon dioxide.

The word equation for the breakdown of baking soda when it is heated is:

sodium hydrogencarbonate $\xrightarrow{\text{heat}}$ sodium carbonate + water + carbon dioxide

The word equation for damp baking powder releasing carbon dioxide is:

sodium hydrogencarbonate + tartaric acid $\longrightarrow$ sodium tartrate + water + carbon dioxide

---

Big bases

Some of the bases and alkalis that you use in school laboratories are produced in huge amounts on an industrial scale. These include calcium oxide, sodium hydroxide and ammonia.

Calcium oxide

Calcium oxide is made by heating calcium carbonate strongly. Rocks such as limestone and dolomite are almost pure calcium carbonate and over a hundred million tonnes of calcium oxide are produced from them each year.

> The word equation for making calcium oxide from calcium carbonate is:
>
> calcium carbonate → calcium oxide + carbon dioxide
>
> This is called a decomposition reaction because the calcium carbonate breaks down to form new substances.

Calcium oxide is a base because it **reacts** with acids and **neutralizes** them. It is often called lime. Farmers spread lime on their fields to neutralize excess acid in the soil, helping their crops to grow better. Builders join bricks together using mortar, which is a mixture of lime, sand and water.

This lake in Sweden is polluted by acid rain. The acidity kills the fish and releases poisonous metals from the ground. To reduce the lake's acidity, many thousands of tonnes of calcium oxide powder are sprayed into it.

Cement is made from lime and clay heated together and concrete is a mixture of lime, sand, small stones and water. Calcium oxide is also used to purify iron and steel. It reacts with acidic impurities in the molten iron, forming waste that is easily removed.

Sodium hydroxide

Sodium hydroxide is made by passing electricity through concentrated sodium chloride solution. The electricity splits the sodium chloride into its two **elements**. Sodium forms at the negative electrode, where it reacts with water to form sodium hydroxide and hydrogen gas. Meanwhile, chlorine gas forms at the positive electrode. This is easy to do in the laboratory, but harder to do on an industrial scale because hydrogen and chlorine will react together if they meet. Over forty million tonnes of sodium hydroxide are made each year. It has all sorts of uses, including the manufacture of paper, artificial fibres and chemicals, as well as for neutralizing the sulphuric acid used by oil refineries.

Ammonia

Ammonia is made using the Haber process. Nitrogen and hydrogen are forced to react together at two hundred times atmospheric pressure. The rate of the reaction is increased using an iron **catalyst** and by raising the temperature to about 450 °C.

The word equation for the Haber process is:

$$nitrogen + hydrogen \rightleftharpoons ammonia$$

This reaction does not go to completion. It is reversible, so we use the $\rightleftharpoons$ symbol instead of an arrow.

Over a hundred million tonnes of ammonia are made each year. Most of it is used in **fertilizers**, but it has many other uses that include the manufacture of explosives, plastics and artificial fibres such as nylon.

Big acids

The acids that you use in school laboratories are also produced in huge amounts on an industrial scale.

Nitric acid

Nitric acid is made by the Ostwald process. Ammonia and air are passed over a hot platinum-rhodium **catalyst**, producing nitrogen monoxide gas and steam. Then the nitrogen monoxide **reacts** with water and more oxygen to form nitric acid.

The word equations for some of the stages in the Ostwald process are:

ammonia + oxygen → nitrogen monoxide + steam

nitrogen monoxide + oxygen + water → nitric acid

About sixty million tonnes of nitric acid are made each year. Most of it is used to produce ammonium nitrate, a **compound** found in **fertilizers** and explosives. Nitric acid is also used to make dyes, plastics and explosives, such as nitroglycerine and trinitrotoluene (TNT).

Sulphuric acid

Sulphuric acid is made by the Contact process, which happens in three stages. Sulphur is burned in air to produce sulphur dioxide gas. Then, at a temperature of 450 °C, twice normal atmospheric pressure and using a catalyst called vanadium pentoxide, it is reacted with more air to make sulphur trioxide gas. Finally sulphur trioxide reacts with water to make sulphuric acid.

More sulphuric acid is made than any other chemical – about one hundred and fifty million tonnes world-wide each year! Most of it goes to make fertilizers, but it is also used to make plastics, paints and explosives.

Phosphoric acid

Phosphoric acid is made by reacting phosphate rock with sulphuric acid. Nearly all of the thirty-five million tonnes made each year are used to make fertilizers. However, phosphoric acid has other uses, that include making water softeners for detergents and rust-proofing steel. It is also used to flavour cola drinks.

Hydrochloric acid

Hydrochloric acid is usually made as a by-product of other chemical processes, although hydrogen and chlorine can be reacted together to make hydrogen chloride gas. This is cooled and dissolved in water to make hydrochloric acid. Hydrochloric acid is used to clean metals and circuit boards, as well as making bleaches, dyes and solvents.

◄ *Hydrogen gas is made when metals react with water or acids. Here you can see lots of tiny bubbles of hydrogen being released when zinc reacts with hydrochloric acid.*

41

Hydrogen in complex molecules

When hydrogen **atoms** join to atoms like oxygen and sulphur they form simple **molecules**, but when they **bond** with carbon atoms they can make very complex molecules. This is because carbon atoms often join together to make long chains, branches and rings. Molecules made from hydrogen and carbon atoms are called hydrocarbons.

Hydrocarbons from oil and natural gas

Nearly all the hydrocarbons we use come from oil and natural gas. These are usually deep underground and have to be drilled. Oil is a mixture of many different hydrocarbons, including solids and gases dissolved in a thick mixture of liquids. The crude oil must be separated into different parts, or fractions, at an oil refinery so that we can use them.

A fishy tale

Millions of years ago, sea creatures died and were buried under layers of mineral sediments. Their bodies did not rot because oxygen could not reach them. Instead, they were squashed by the weight of the sediments and heated. Eventually the mineral sediments became rock and the remains turned into oil and natural gas.

The different hydrocarbons are separated from each other in a metal tower called a fractionating column. The fractions from the top of the column are gases with very small molecules, those from the middle are liquids with medium-sized molecules and those at the bottom are solids with big molecules. Each fraction contains hydrocarbons called alkanes.

Alkanes

The carbon atoms of alkanes are joined to each other with single bonds. The fraction from the top of the fractionating column contains the fuel gases: methane, ethane, propane and butane. Methane, CH_4, is the simplest alkane – each molecule contains four hydrogen atoms joined to a carbon atom. Natural gas is mostly methane with some ethane.

Natural gas is an important fuel for power stations, factories and homes. Propane and butane are used in bottled gases, such as camping gas.

◀ *Butane gas, extracted from crude oil at oil refineries and stored under pressure in metal cylinders, is widely used by campers for cooking and lighting.*

How many bonds?

When two carbon atoms join together using one chemical bond, it is called a single bond. Carbon atoms can also join together using two or three chemical bonds, called double bonds and triple bonds respectively.

Most of the other fractions are liquids that are used to make lubricating oil and fuels. Petrol and diesel oil are important fuels for cars and lorries, while kerosene is used in jet fuel. Fuel oil is a very thick liquid utilized by ships and oil-fired power stations.

Very long alkanes, such as paraffin waxes and bitumen, are solid at room temperature. Each molecule of bitumen contains over fifty carbon atoms and over a hundred hydrogen atoms. Candles and polishes are made from paraffin waxes and bitumen is used to surface roads.

◀ *Jet aircraft are powered by kerosene, a liquid fuel extracted from crude oil.*

Plastic and margarine

Medium-sized alkanes, like octane, are often more useful than big alkanes like bitumen. However crude oil contains too few medium-sized alkanes and too many big alkanes. Some of the big alkanes are broken into smaller alkanes using a process called cracking, which involves heating them under pressure or passing them over a **catalyst**. Cracking also produces alkenes, a different type of hydrocarbon.

Alkenes

In an alkene **molecule**, two or more of the carbon **atoms** are joined together using double **bonds** instead of single bonds. This makes alkenes more **reactive** than alkanes. Hydrogen, bromine, water and other chemicals can join on to alkenes wherever there is a double bond. Alkenes can even join on to each other to make really long molecules, called addition polymers.

Testing for alkenes

Bromine mixed with water is used to test if hydrocarbons are alkanes or alkenes. Bromine water stays brown when it is shaken with an alkane, but becomes colourless when mixed with an alkene. This is because bromine atoms add on to the alkene molecules.

Addition polymers

There are lots of addition polymers, depending on the alkene used to make them. The simplest alkene is ethene, C_2H_4. When ethene molecules join end to end, they make poly(ethene), which is used to make polythene bags. The next simplest alkene is propene, C_3H_6. When propene molecules join end to end they make poly(propene), which is used to make tough polypropylene ropes and crates. Styrene is a more complex alkene with a ring of carbon and hydrogen atoms. When styrene molecules join end to end it makes polystyrene, which is used for fast-food containers and TV cabinets.

▲
Polystyrene is a plastic made from a complex molecule containing rings of carbon and hydrogen atoms. It is widely used to make packaging and containers for food.

Margarine

Hydrogen can add on to the double bonds in alkenes. When this happens, it converts the alkene into an alkane. This might seem pointless, but it is an important step in making margarine.

Oils and fats are made from molecules with long chains of carbon atoms. If all the carbon atoms are joined together by single bonds, the fat is called 'saturated'. Saturated fats, such as lard, are hard solids at room temperature. If some of the carbon atoms are joined together by double bonds, the fat is called 'unsaturated'. Unsaturated fats are soft solids or runny oils, such as vegetable oil.

If hydrogen is added to vegetable oils, they become more saturated. This makes them solid, rather than liquid. Margarine manufacturers react vegetable oils with hydrogen gas using a nickel catalyst, which converts some of the double bonds into single bonds. When the ingredients include 'hydrogenated vegetable oil' this is what it means. The different **products** from the reaction are blended together to make different margarines for cooking or spreading.

Ethanol and esters

The liquid, ethanol, C_2H_5OH, is the best known member of a whole family of **compounds** named alcohols and is commonly called alcohol. Around thirty billion litres of ethanol are made in the world each year, but most of this does not end up in alcoholic drinks! Ethanol is a very good fuel and is used as a solvent in deodorants, perfumes and ink.

The hydroxyl group

Every alcohol contains a 'hydroxyl group', OH, which is an oxygen atom and a hydrogen atom joined together. Without it, alcohols would not be alcohols at all.

Making ethanol

Ethanol can be made from ethene, an alkene formed by cracking oil fractions. To make ethanol, the ethene must be mixed with steam at sixty times atmospheric pressure (atm), heated to 300 °C and then passed over a **catalyst**.

The word equation for making ethanol from ethene and steam is:

$$\text{ethene + steam} \xrightarrow{\text{300 °C, 60atm}} \text{ethanol}$$

Phosphoric acid stuck on to solid pellets is used as a catalyst.

Ethanol can also be made from sugar. Yeast is a type of single-celled fungi that breaks up sugar, using fermentation. This process involves natural catalysts, called **enzymes**. Fermentation produces ethanol and carbon dioxide gas. Almost anything containing sugar can be used for fermentation, including grape juice, sugar cane and corn.

The word equation for fermentation is:

$$\text{glucose} \xrightarrow{\text{enzymes in yeast}} \text{ethanol} + \text{carbon dioxide}$$

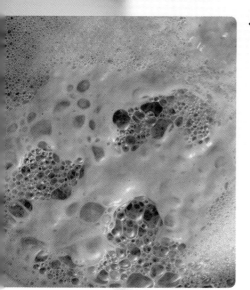

◀ Yeast can ferment sugar solution to produce the ethanol contained in beer and wine. The reaction also produces bubbles of carbon dioxide gas, which causes froth to form on the surface of the sugar solution.

Ethanol the biofuel

Crude oil is a limited resource because it takes millions of years to form and once it is used up it will be gone for good. Ethanol is a 'biofuel' that can be made from various crops that can be replaced. Huge amounts of ethanol are made in Brazil from sugar cane and in the USA from corn. Gasohol, a mixture of 10 per cent ethanol and 90 per cent petrol, fuels many cars in Brazil, while in the USA a mixture of 85 per cent ethanol and 15 per cent petrol, called E85, does a similar job.

Fruity smells

If a bottle of wine is left open, the ethanol in it **reacts** with oxygen in the air, turning it into ethanoic acid, CH_3COOH. This is a weak acid that belongs to a family of compounds named carboxylic acids. Vinegar is 4 per cent ethanoic acid, which is why it has a sharp taste.

When an alcohol and a carboxylic acid react together, they make water and a complex substance called an ester. Esters have fruity tastes and smells and are found naturally in fruit and flowers. Different combinations of alcohols and carboxylic acids make different esters. Manufactures add esters to cosmetics and shampoos to give them a 'natural' fragrance and esters are used as artificial flavours in yogurts and other foods.

Carbohydrates everywhere

Animals obtain their food by eating plants or other animals, but plants make their own through a process called photosynthesis. Using the energy from sunlight, water is made to **react** with carbon dioxide to produce glucose and oxygen. Glucose is just one sugar in a large range of **compounds** that includes big, complex **molecules** such as starch. These compounds are called carbohydrates because they contain carbon, hydrogen and oxygen.

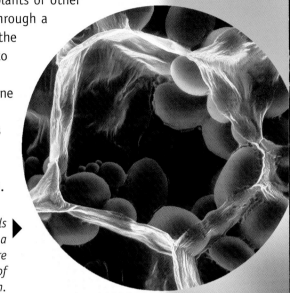

These highly magnified potato cells contain rounded granules of starch, a complex carbohydrate used as a food store by plants. Carbohydrates are compounds of carbon, hydrogen and oxygen.

The word equation for photosynthesis is:

$$\text{carbon dioxide + water} \xrightarrow{\text{sunlight}} \text{glucose + oxygen}$$

Photosynthesis happens in tiny green bodies in plant cells called chloroplasts.

Sugar, sugar

Glucose and galactose are two simple sugars. They both have the formula $C_6H_{12}O_6$, but they are not identical. Other simple sugars also have the same chemical formula but different arrangements of their **atoms.** Two molecules of a simple sugar can join together to make more complex sugars. For example, glucose added to galactose forms lactose, which is found in milk, while glucose attached to fructose makes sucrose, which is cane sugar.

Starch is made when thousands of glucose molecules join together. Plants store their food as tiny starch granules in their cells. Glucose is the main sugar in our blood, but we store it in the liver and muscles as glycogen. This is another complex molecule made from thousands of glucose molecules that are joined together in a different way to the molecules in starch.

Blood groups

In 1901 Karl Landsteiner first discovered that there are different types of blood, which he named A, B and O. Each blood group has a different chain of sugar molecules on the surface of the red blood cells.

Cellulose – the tough stuff

Cellulose is a tough molecule found in plant cell walls that is also made from glucose molecules joined together in yet another way. We can digest starch, but not cellulose because we do not have the necessary **enzymes**. However, many fungi and bacteria do have these enzymes and use cellulose for food. Cows and other ruminants have bacteria in their stomachs that digest the cellulose in plants for them.

The cellulose in wood is used to make paper and an artificial fibre called rayon. To make rayon the cellulose is turned into a syrupy substance called viscose by reacting it with sodium hydroxide and carbon disulphide. The viscose is sprayed through fine holes into dilute sulphuric acid. This **neutralizes** the sodium hydroxide and turns the viscose into threads of rayon. Rayon is used for clothing, carpets and bandages.

▶ *These cattle have no problem digesting cellulose, the tough carbohydrate molecule found in the cell walls of grass and other plants. We do not have the enzymes needed to digest cellulose, so it forms roughage in our diet that helps food pass through our intestine properly.*

The stuff of life

Hydrogen **atoms** are found in some very complex **molecules**, such as deoxyribonucleic acid (DNA) and proteins. Many of them are involved in special chemical **bonds**, called 'hydrogen bonds'.

What are hydrogen bonds?

Hydrogen bonds form between a hydrogen atom and an atom of fluorine, oxygen or nitrogen. They can form between two molecules or parts of a large molecule. Hydrogen bonds are stronger than most other bonds between molecules. They increase the boiling points of small molecules and keep complex molecules in the correct shape.

Thank you, hydrogen bonds!

Molecules attracted to each other by weak bonds are easily separated by a little heat energy. As a result, they have low boiling points and are usually gases at room temperature. Hydrogen, oxygen and nitrogen are all gases at room temperature because they are made from small molecules, but what about water?

Water, H_2O, is also a small molecule. It only contains three atoms and two of those are the smallest in the **periodic table**. This means that water ought to be a gas at room temperature, but it is a liquid instead. This is because hydrogen bonds form between water molecules and extra heat energy is needed to separate them, giving water a high boiling point. Without hydrogen bonds, the boiling point of water would be about −70 °C, not 100 °C. The oceans, lakes and rivers would all boil away and life as we know it could not exist.

Get into shape with hydrogen bonds

DNA contains all the information a cell needs to function. It is a very complex molecule and human DNA can be 7cm long! Luckily, DNA is tightly rolled up to fit into the nuclei of our cells. It is made from two long molecules or strands that twist around each other. They form a special spiral, called a double helix, that is held together by hydrogen bonds.

Proteins

Proteins are large molecules. There are many different types, which have a huge variety of jobs. Muscle, hair and skin contain proteins. A protein called albumin is in egg white. Hydrogen bonds help to keep albumin molecules in shape. If egg white is cooked, the heat breaks the hydrogen bonds in the albumin and it becomes solid and white. Other proteins form natural **catalysts** called **enzymes**, such as those in yeast that convert sugar into ethanol. These are also sensitive to heat.

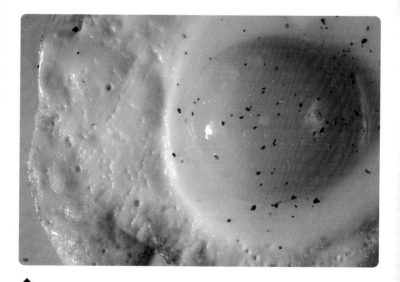

▲
Weak chemical bonds called hydrogen bonds help to keep proteins in their correct shapes. When an egg is cooked, the hydrogen bonds in its proteins are broken. This changes the egg white from a runny, almost see-through substance to a white solid.

Enzymes control the chemical **reactions** in our cells, but are damaged by changes in pH and temperatures above 45 °C. 'Biological' detergents contain enzymes to break down the fats in greasy stains. However, clothes have to be washed at low temperatures otherwise the hydrogen bonds in the enzymes would break. This changes their shape and stops them from working.

◀ *DNA is the complex molecule that controls the growth and development of all living things. In the model (opposite) of a small section of DNA, the hydrogen atoms are the white balls.*

Metal or non-metal?

Hydrogen is an unusual **element** in many ways. It is often placed alone in the **periodic table** and even when it is positioned above lithium in **group** 1, it does not really belong there. We usually think of hydrogen as a non-metal, but it does have some properties of metals.

Properties of metals and non-metals

The table gives a summary of some of the typical properties of metals and non-metals.

Metals	Non-metals
shiny	dull
high melting and boiling points	low melting and boiling points
High **density** (they feel heavy)	low density (they feel light)
strong	weak
malleable (bend without breaking)	brittle (break when bent or hit)
ductile (they make wires)	not ductile
good conductors of heat and electricity	good insulators
form positive **ions** in reactions	form negative ions in reactions
oxides are bases	oxides are acids

Hydrogen the metal

Hydrogen behaves like a metal whenever acids dissolve in water and form positively charged hydrogen ions, H^+. Scientists have also discovered that, like metals, hydrogen can be made to conduct electricity. Under extreme conditions, of more than a million times atmospheric pressure, hydrogen turns into a liquid that conducts electricity. At even higher pressures it turns into a solid that also conducts electricity.

Hydrogen the non-metal

Hydrogen is a gas at room temperature and a good insulator. Just like a non-metal, it **reacts** with other non-metals to form **molecules**. We have seen many examples of these molecules in this book, such as ammonia, NH_3 and methane, CH_4. The really complicated molecules like DNA, proteins, plastics and sugars all contain hydrogen **atoms** joined to non-metal atoms.

A little of both?

Metal oxides are bases and non-metal oxides are acids when they are dissolved in water, but what about hydrogen? Water or hydrogen oxide, H_2O, is neutral.

Non-metals such as chlorine and oxygen form negatively charged ions in reactions with metals. Chlorine forms chloride ions, Cl^- and oxygen forms oxide ions, O^{2-}. Similarly hydrogen forms hydride ions, H^-, when it reacts with reactive metals like lithium, making lithium hydride, LiH.

There are even more hydrides, such as lithium aluminium hydride, $LiAlH_4$ and sodium borohydride, $NaBH_4$. These are used as 'reducing agents' by the chemical industry and can

either remove oxygen atoms from molecules or add hydrogen atoms. They can change carboxylic acids back to alcohols, so ethanoic acid turns back into ethanol. They can also convert carboxylic acids into aldehydes, which are **compounds** with a sickly-sweet smell. Methanal, HCHO, is an aldehyde used in sheep dips and as a preservative for biology specimens because it is a poisonous gas, so solutions of it will kill bacteria, insects and fungi.

◀ *Methanal is a rather smelly compound of carbon, hydrogen and oxygen used to preserve biology specimens like this brain.*

CHAPTER 8

Here comes the Sun

Hydrogen is the major **element** in the Sun and is a very flammable gas that burns easily in air. However, there is no air in space, so what is happening in the Sun? The answer to this question is that all the energy given off comes from **nuclear reactions** not chemical **reactions**.

Nuclear reactions

Chemical reactions happen when **atoms** swap or share **electrons**, but nuclear reactions occur when an atom's **nucleus** actually changes. The Sun uses a type of reaction, called nuclear fusion. This arises when the nuclei of two atoms crash into each other with so much energy that they stick together. The reaction forms the nucleus of a larger atom and releases lots of energy and **radiation**.

Fusion in the Sun

Fusion in the Sun happens in several stages, but overall four hydrogen-1 nuclei join together to make one helium-4 nucleus. The mass of a helium-4 nucleus is slightly less than the mass of four hydrogen-1 nuclei. Some of the left-over mass goes to make **subatomic particles** called neutrinos and positrons, but the rest is converted into energy.

Einstein's equation

Albert Einstein was a German physicist who discovered an equation that connects energy and mass. In his famous equation, $E=mc^2$, E stands for energy, m stands for mass and c stands for the speed of light. As the speed of light is very fast (300,000,000 m/s), it means that a tiny mass can be converted into an enormous amount of energy.

Seven hundred million tonnes of hydrogen undergoes nuclear fusion in the Sun every second, producing nearly four billion billion megawatts of energy. On average, each square metre of the Earth receives 1.36 kW of energy from the Sun. The Sun provides light needed for plants to photosynthesize and the heat that drives the water cycle. It also keeps the Earth warm enough for life to exist.

Without the Sun, the Earth would be frozen and lifeless. Plants such as this barley would not get the light they need to make their food. They would die and eventually we would all starve.

There goes the Sun

Our Sun is a 'yellow dwarf' star. It has been shining for nearly five billion years and has enough hydrogen for another five billion years. When the Sun begins to run out of hydrogen, gravity will make the Sun's core smaller, causing it to heat up. Eventually it will be hot enough to join helium nuclei together, making the nuclei of bigger atoms, such as carbon. Unfortunately, it will also make the outer layers of the Sun expand. They will expand so much, that the Sun will become a 'red giant', swallowing the Earth and boiling it away.

For more information on the Sun see the table on page 62.

Our Sun is a gigantic nuclear fireball fuelled by hydrogen. Its surface is constantly moving, and every so often huge solar flares erupt outwards and return to the surface. The one you can see here is over half a million kilometres across.

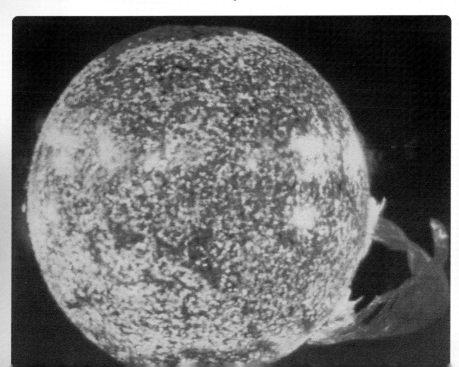

Copying nature

Our Sun uses hydrogen to produce immense amounts of energy by nuclear fusion. On Earth, the water **molecules** in the oceans contain enough hydrogen to power the Sun for seven years! Not suprisingly scientists are keen to copy what happens in the Sun. The first attempts at nuclear fusion on Earth were really very successful – except they made huge explosions rather than electricity.

Hydrogen bombs

Hydrogen bombs are incredibly powerful. Like the Sun, they work by making hydrogen **nuclei** join together. In 1952, the US tested the first hydrogen bomb at Eniwetok Atoll in the Pacific Ocean. The bomb was codenamed 'Mike' for 'megaton' and used liquid deuterium chilled with huge refrigeration equipment. Its devastating power destroyed an island and left a crater nearly 2 km wide and 50 m deep!

This fiery mushroom-shaped cloud was caused by the testing of a hydrogen bomb over Bikini Atoll in 1954. Hydrogen bombs are incredibly powerful – this explosion had the same power as eleven million tonnes of explosive.

Deuterium and tritium on Earth

*An American scientist called Harold Urey discovered deuterium in 1931. Water containing deuterium (hydrogen-2) **atoms** instead of ordinary hydrogen-1 atoms is called 'heavy water'. Tritium (hydrogen-3) is very rare on Earth. Cosmic rays from space cause it to form in the upper atmosphere and it was first made artificially in 1934. Tritium is **radioactive** and was once used in luminous digital watch dials.*

Modern hydrogen bombs work by forcing deuterium and tritium nuclei together. Liquid hydrogen is difficult to handle and tritium is rare and radioactive, so a solid called lithium deuteride is used instead. This is lithium hydride, LiH, made from deuterium instead of ordinary hydrogen-1.

An atomic bomb is used as a detonator, providing the energy and **radiation** needed to get the fusion reaction going. The radiation causes some of the lithium in the lithium deuteride to break apart to form tritium. In the tremendous heat and pressure caused by the detonator, nuclei join together and release huge amounts of energy. Tritium nuclei join with deuterium nuclei and deuterium nuclei also join together. The whole process takes about half a millionth of a second and would cause unimaginable disaster!

Atomic bombs
Atomic bombs use nuclear fission instead of nuclear fusion. This is when the nucleus of a large atom, such as uranium, breaks apart, forming nuclei of smaller atoms and releasing lots of energy and radiation. 'Little Boy', the first atomic bomb to be used in a war, was exploded on 6 August 1945, during World War II. It killed over sixty thousand people in the Japanese city of Hiroshima.

Hot doughnuts
Attempts to use nuclear fusion to generate electricity have been less successful. Heating the mixture of deuterium and tritium to very high temperatures, while keeping it inside the reactor is a major problem. Experimental reactors, called tokamaks, are shaped like hollow doughnuts. They use powerful magnetic fields to keep the hot mixture together and away from the walls. Research continues, but so far more energy is used than made. It may be years before all the problems are solved, but when they are we will have an almost limitless supply of energy – until the Sun turns into a red dwarf!

Find out more about hydrogen

The table below contains some information about the properties of hydrogen.

Element	Symbol	Atomic number	Melting point (°C)	Boiling point (°C)	State at 25 °C	Density at 25 °C (g/cm³)
hydrogen	H	1	−259	−253	gas	0.00115

The table below contains some information about the properties of hydrogen **isotopes**.

Isotope	Symbol	Mass number	Half-life	Radiation	Per cent of natural hydrogen atoms
hydrogen-1 (protium)	^1_1H	1	stable	none	99.989
hydrogen-2 (deuterium)	^2_1H	2	stable	none	0.011
hydrogen-3 (tritium)	^3_1H	3	12.3 years	beta	0

Beta **radiation**, β, is caused by high-energy **electrons** shot out from the **nucleus**.

Compounds

These tables show you the chemical formulae of most of the **compounds** mentioned in this book. For example, ammonia has the formula NH_3. This means it is made from one nitrogen **atom** and three hydrogen atoms, joined together by chemical **bonds**.

Calcium compounds

Calcium compounds	formula
calcium carbonate	$CaCO_3$
calcium chloride	$CaCl_2$
calcium hydrogencarbonate	$Ca(HCO_3)_2$
calcium oxide	CaO
calcium phosphate	$Ca_3(PO_4)_2$
calcium sulphate	$CaSO_4$

Carbon compounds	formula
butane	C_4H_{10}
butanol	C_4H_9OH
carbon dioxide	CO_2
carbon disulphide	CS_2
ethane	C_2H_6
ethanoic acid	CH_3COOH
ethanol	C_2H_5OH
ethene	C_2H_4
glucose	$C_6H_{12}O_6$
methanal	HCHO
methane	CH_4
octanol	$C_8H_{17}OH$
octyl ethanoate	$CH_3COOC_8H_{17}$
pentanol	$C_5H_{11}OH$
pentyl ethanoate	$CH_3COOC_5H_{11}$
propane	C_3H_8
propene	C_3H_6

Carbon compounds

Lithium compounds	formula
lithium aluminium hydride	$LiAlH_4$
lithium hydride	LiH

Lithium compounds

Nitrogen compounds	formula
ammonia	NH_3
ammonium chloride	NH_4Cl
ammonium nitrate	NH_4NO_3
nitrogen monoxide	NO
nitroglycerine	$C_3H_5(ONO_2)_3$
trinitrotoluene	$CH_3C_6H_2(NO_2)_3$

Nitrogen compounds

Find out more continued

Sodium compounds

Sodium compounds	formula
sodium borohydride	$NaBH_4$
sodium carbonate	Na_2CO_3
sodium chloride	$NaCl$
sodium hydrogencarbonate	$NaHCO_3$
sodium hydroxide	$NaOH$
sodium tartrate	$Na_2C_4H_4O_6$

Sulphur compounds

Sulphur compounds	formula
sulphur dioxide	SO_2
sulphur trioxide	SO_3

Other compounds

Other compounds	formula
aluminium oxide	Al_2O_3
cobalt chloride	$CoCl_2$
copper oxide	CuO
magnesium chloride	$MgCl_2$
potassium hydroxide	KOH
vanadium pentoxide	V_2O_5
hydrogen oxide (water)	H_2O
zinc sulphate	$ZnSO_4$

Acids

Acids	formula
carbonic acid	H_2CO_3
hydrochloric acid	HCl
nitric acid	HNO_3
phosphoric acid	H_3PO_4
sulphuric acid	H_2SO_4
tartaric acid	$C_4H_6O_6$

Glossary

alloy mixture of two or more metals or mixture of a metal and a non-metal. Alloys are often more useful than the pure metal on its own.

atom smallest particle of an element that has the properties of that element. Atoms contain smaller particles called subatomic particles.

atomic number number of protons in the nucleus of an atom. No two elements have the same atomic number.

bond force that join atoms together

catalyst substance that speeds up reactions without getting used up

compound substance made from the atoms of two or more elements, joined together by chemical bonds. Compounds can be broken down into simpler substances and have different properties from the elements in them. For example, water is a liquid at room temperature, but it is made from two gases, hydrogen and oxygen.

density mass of a substance compared to its volume. To work out the density of a substance, divide its mass by its volume. Substances with a high density feel very heavy for their size.

electron subatomic particle with a negative electric charge. Electrons are found around the nucleus of an atom.

element substance made from one type of atom. Elements cannot be broken down into simpler substances. All substances are made from one or more elements.

enzyme catalyst made by living things. They are made from proteins and control the chemical reactions that happen in living things.

extract remove a chemical from a mixture of chemicals

fertilizer chemical that gives plants the elements they need for healthy growth

fossil fuel fuel that is formed from the ancient remains of plants and animals. Coal, oil and natural gas are fossil fuels.

group vertical column of elements in the periodic table. Elements in a group have similar properties.

ion charged particle made when atoms lose or gain electrons. If a metal atom loses electrons it becomes a positive ion. If a non-metal atom gains electrons it becomes a negative ion.

isotope atom of an element with the same number of protons and electrons, but different numbers of neutrons

mass number number of protons added to the number of neutrons in the nucleus of an atom

molecule smallest unit of an element or compound that exists by itself. A molecule is usually made from two or more atoms joined together.

neutralize when an acid and an alkali or a base react together the solution made is neutral, which means it is not acidic or alkaline.

neutron subatomic particle with no electric charge. Neutrons are found in the nucleus of an atom.

nuclear reaction reaction involving the nucleus of an atom. Radiation is produced in nuclear reactions.

nucleus part of an atom made from protons and neutrons. It has a positive electric charge and is found at the centre of the atom.

period horizontal row of elements in the periodic table

periodic table table in which all the known elements are arranged into groups and periods

product substance made in a chemical reaction

proton subatomic particle with a positive electric charge. Protons are found in the nucleus of an atom.

radiation energy or particles given off when an atom decays or breaks down

radioactive describes a substance that can produce radiation

reaction chemical change that produces new substances

salt chemical formed when an acid is neutralized

spectrum colours that make up a ray of light. Different colours of light have different spectra.

subatomic particle particle smaller than an atom, such as a proton, neutron or electron

welding joining two or more metals together, usually by heating them

Sun facts

The Sun contains huge amounts of hydrogen. This table contains some information about the Sun.

	Actual amount	**A comparison to help**
distance from the earth	149,600,000 km	London to New York (and back) thirteen thousand times
diameter of the Sun	1,390,000 km	London to New York (and back) one hundred and twenty-four times
mass of the Sun	1,989 billion billion billion tonnes	three hundred and thirty thousand times the mass of the earth
surface temperature	5530 °C	three times the melting point of iron
inside temperature	15,600,000 °C	eight thousand six hundred times the melting point of iron
energy output	386 billion billion megawatts	a hundred billion times the power output of the largest coal-fired power station in Europe
mass of hydrogen fuel used	7,000,000,000 tonnes per second	**extracting** and using the hydrogen from a ball of water 2 km in diameter every second

Timeline

discovers a flammable gas and calls it 'inflammable air'	1766	Henry Cavendish
names it hydrogen. Discovers that hydrogen burns in air to produce water.	1783	Antoine Lavoisier
discovers hydrogen in the Sun by studying the **spectrum** of sunlight	1862	Anders Ångström
deuterium discovered	1931	Harold Urey
tritium discovered	1934	Lord Rutherford
invention of the gas battery, the first hydrogen fuel cell	1842	William Grove
test detonation of the world's first hydrogen bomb in the Pacific Ocean	1952	USA

Further reading and useful websites

Books

Knapp, Brian, *The Elements* series, particularly, *Hydrogen and the Noble Gases* (Atlantic Europe Publishing Co., 1996)

Oxlade, Chris, *Chemicals in Action* series, particularly, *Acids and Bases* (Heinemann Library, 2002)

Oxlade, Chris, *Chemicals in Action* series, particularly, *Elements and Compounds* (Heinemann Library, 2002)

Websites

WebElements™
http://www.webelements.com
An interactive periodic table crammed with information and photographs.

DiscoverySchool
http://school.discovery.com/clipart/
Help for science projects and homework. Free science clip art is available.

Proton Don
http://www.funbrain.com/periodic
The fun periodic table quiz!

BBC Science
http://www.bbc.co.uk/science
Quizzes, news, information and games about all areas of science.

Creative Chemistry
http://www.creative-chemistry.org.uk
An interactive chemistry site with fun practical activities, quizzes, puzzles and more.

Index

Titles in the *Periodic Table* series include:

Hardback   0 431 16995 0

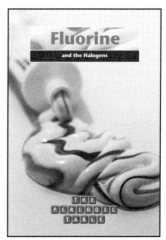

Hardback   0 431 16997 7

Hardback   0 431 16998 5

Hardback   0 431 16996 9

Hardback   0 431 16994 2

Hardback   0 431 16999 3

Find out about the other titles in this series on our website www.heinemann.co.uk/library